★ ★ ★

A PRIMARY SOURCE HISTORY
OF THE UNITED STATES

THE GREAT DEPRESSION AND WORLD WAR II

1929–1949

George E. Stanley

WORLD ALMANAC® LIBRARY

Please visit our web site at: www.worldalmanaclibrary.com
For a free color catalog describing World Almanac® Library's list of high-quality books and multimedia programs, call 1-800-848-2928 (USA) or 1-800-387-3178 (Canada). World Almanac® Library's fax: (414) 332-3567.

Library of Congress Cataloging-in-Publication Data available upon request from publisher. Fax (414) 336-0157 for the attention of the Publishing Records Department.

ISBN 0-8368-5829-8 (lib. bdg.)
ISBN 0-8368-5838-7 (softcover)

First published in 2005 by
World Almanac® Library
330 West Olive Street, Suite 100
Milwaukee, WI 53212 USA

Produced by Byron Preiss Visual Publications Inc.
Project Editor: Susan Hoe
Designer: Marisa Gentile
World Almanac® Library editor: Alan Wachtel
World Almanac® Library art direction: Tammy West

Picture acknowledgements:
The Granger Collection: Cover (upper left, lower left, upper right). clipart.com: p. 5.
Library of Congress: Cover (lower right), pp. 4, 6, 8, 13, 15, 16, 17, 18, 20, 21, 23, 24, 26, 27, 29, 31, 32, 33, 35, 41, 43. U.S. Marine Corp.: p. 38.

Printed in the United States of America

1 2 3 4 5 6 7 8 9 09 08 07 06 05

Dr. George E. Stanley is a professor at Cameron University in Lawton, Oklahoma. He has authored more than eighty books for young readers, many in the field of history and science. Dr. Stanley recently completed a series of history books on famous Americans, including *Geronimo, Andrew Jackson, Harry S. Truman,* and *Mr. Rogers.*

CONTENTS

Through the examination of authentic historical documents, including charters, diaries, journals, letters, speeches, and other written records, each title in *A Primary Source History of the United States* offers a unique perspective on the events that shaped the United States. In addition to providing important historical information, each document serves as a piece of living history that opens a window into the kinds of thinking and modes of expression that characterized the various epochs of American history.

Note: To facilitate the reading of older documents, the modern-day spelling of certain words is used.

CHAPTER 1

Hard Times

1929–1933

When the stock market crashed during the last week of October 1929, millionaires became paupers overnight. Some men who had lost all of their invested money committed suicide by jumping out of skyscrapers.

Even though President Herbert Hoover and business leaders such as John D. Rockefeller said that the economy was fundamentally sound, most Americans didn't believe them, and it was impossible to stem the panic in the stock market.

When people stopped spending money, companies cut back production and fired employees. The total value of goods and services, known as the gross national product, fell by more than thirty percent between 1929 and 1932. Farmers burned their crops and poured milk on highways as a protest against falling prices, and thousands of out-of-work city dwellers stood in long lines for bread and soup.

President Hoover tried to revitalize the economy with the Reconstruction

▼ Bread lines were a common sight in New York City during the Great Depression.

Finance Corporation, which provided money to financial institutions for loans. The Glass-Steagall Act made it easier for companies to get credit. The Emergency Relief and the Construction Act provided money for local, state, and federal projects. But nothing seemed to work.

Americans longed for the "good old days" of prosperity. To get their minds off the bleakness that surrounded them, they went to the movies to enjoy happy musicals and sophisticated comedies—and movie critics helped them decide which ones to see by writing reviews in such magazines as *The Literary Digest* and the *Hollywood Reporter*.

REVIEWS OF THE MOVIE *LIBELED LADY*: 1936

The Literary Digest:
The cinema season's most piquant and daring comedy also is the funniest. It is Libeled Lady, a Metro-Goldwyn-Mayer production employing such audacious talent as Jean Harlow, William Powell, Myrna Loy and Spencer Tracy.

Hollywood Reporter:
Count on an hour and a half of almost continuous laughter ... in a bubbling French-type farce, tailored in the smartest American mode, that sparkles and twists. And enough witty dialog to stock five ordinary comedies.

Spencer Tracy was one of the stars in the 1936 movie *Libeled Lady*, which provided a happy diversion for audiences during the depression. ▶

THE BONUS ARMY

At the end of World War I, the United States government passed a bill that would give veterans a cash bonus in 1945 (to be a kind of retirement benefit), but in the summer of 1932, several thousand former soldiers and their families marched on Washington, D.C., demanding early payment. They called themselves the

"Bonus Army," and they lived in tents at Anacostia Flats while they waited to see what the government would do. When the "early payment" proposal was defeated in the Senate, some of the people went home, but thousands of others protested up and down Pennsylvania Avenue for several days.

President Hoover considered the Bonus Army a threat to public safety, and he ordered everyone removed from the tent city. The army, under the command of General Douglas MacArthur, confronted unarmed veterans and their families with bayonets, tear gas, machine guns, and tanks. The men hurled back stones and bricks. What followed shocked the entire nation. Men and women were chased down by soldiers on horses, and children were tear-gassed. After seeing American soldiers attacking American citizens, most people said they would never vote to reelect Hoover as president. The Veteran's Bonus Bill, which awarded veterans their benefits, was eventually passed in 1936.

NEW YORK TIMES: JULY 29, 1932

Flames rose high over the desolate Anacostia Flats [in the southeast corner of Washington, D.C.] at midnight tonight, and a pitiful stream of refugee veterans of the World War walked out of their home of the past two months, going they knew not where....

▲ A member of the Bonus Army camps out on the Anacostia Flats with his wife and six children.

INVASION OF MANCHURIA

In order to expand Japan's possessions in China, elements of the Japanese army set off an explosion on the Japanese-owned South Manchurian Railway in 1931 and used this incident as a pretext to occupy all of Manchuria. "We are seeking room that will let us breathe," a Japanese politician said. Even though the seizure of Manchuria violated the Nine-Power Treaty and the Kellogg-Briand Pact, the United States did not have the power to force Japan to withdraw.

The League of Nations did little about the matter except debate.

THE STIMSON DOCTRINE: 1932

The American Government continues confident that the work of the neutral commission recently authorized by the Council of the League of Nations will facilitate an ultimate solution of the difficulties now existing between China and Japan. But in view of the present situation and of its own rights and obligations therein, the American Government deems it to be its duty to notify both the Imperial Japanese Government and the Government of the Chinese Republic that it cannot admit the legality of any situation de facto nor does it intend to recognize any treaty or agreement entered into between those Governments, or agents thereof, which may impair the treaty rights of the United States or its citizens in China, including those which relate to the sovereignty, the independence, or the territorial and administrative integrity of the Republic of China....

— ★ —

Secretary of State Henry Stimson wrote the American response, which declared that the U.S. government would not recognize the changes in China that were imposed by the Japanese. Nevertheless, Japan continued to harass China. In mid-1937, the Sino-Japanese War erupted. The gruesome bombing of Shanghai only intensified anti-Japanese feelings in the United States and set the two countries on a collision course.

FRANKLIN D. ROOSEVELT IS ELECTED

In 1932, the Republicans nominated Hoover for a second term, even though most in the party knew that he wouldn't win the election. Despite Hoover's efforts to revitalize the weak economy, the American people blamed him for the Great Depression. They even called the tarpaper-shack shantytowns—which many people now lived in—"Hoovervilles."

The Democrats nominated Franklin D. Roosevelt, the governor of New York and a distant cousin of Theodore Roosevelt. FDR—as he was popularly known—had served as assistant secretary of the navy under President Wilson. Largely on the basis of his name, Roosevelt had been nominated as the 1920 Democratic vice presidential candidate in an election that Republican candidate Warren G. Harding had won.

In 1921, Roosevelt was stricken with polio, leaving him paralyzed from the waist down, but in 1924, he began a political comeback when he gave an important speech at the Democratic convention, and in 1928 and in 1930, he was elected governor of New York.

During the 1932 presidential campaign, although Roosevelt promised the American people a "new deal," he didn't offer any specific ways his administration would respond to the depression. Instead, he gave several radio speeches in which he talked vaguely about helping the forgotten man at the bottom of the economic pyramid. He felt that government should distribute the nation's wealth more equitably. He also called for reduced federal spending and a balanced budget.

▲ Franklin Roosevelt campaigns from the rear platform of his train during the 1932 presidential election.

Radio would soon play a very important role in Roosevelt's administration. His "fireside chats"—as they became known—allowed the president to explain his plans for the nation's recovery in clear, concise, but never condescending, language. This was a remarkable departure for the presidency. Few presidents had ever dared to speak so frankly to the American people about such complex and important subjects. The fireside chats were down-to-earth appeals to the common man.

ROOSEVELT'S RADIO SPEECH: APRIL 7, 1932

… What we must do is this: To revise our tariff on the basis of a reciprocal exchange of goods, allowing other nations to buy and to pay for our goods by sending us such of their goods as will not seriously throw any of our industries out of balance, and, incidentally, making impossible in this country the continuance of pure monopolies which cause us to pay excessive prices for many of the necessities of life.

Such objectives as these three—restoring farmers' buying power, relief to the small banks and homeowners, and a reconstructed tariff policy—these are only a part of ten or dozen vital factors.

But they seem to be beyond the concern of [Hoover's] Administration which can think in terms only of the top of the social and economic structure. They have sought temporary relief from the top down rather than permanent relief from the bottom up. They have totally failed to plan ahead in a comprehensive way. They have waited until something has cracked and then at the last moment have sought to prevent total collapse.

It is high time to get back to fundamentals. It is high time to admit with courage that we are in the midst of an emergency at least equal to that of war. Let us mobilize to meet it.

❝It is high time to admit with courage that we are in the midst of an emergency at least equal to that of war.❞

CHAPTER 2

Roosevelt and the New Deal

1933–1939

The Twentieth Amendment to the Constitution was ratified in early 1933. It moved the presidential inauguration from March 4 to January 20, because, unlike when the Union was founded, there was no need for a long interval between the time the results of the election were known and the time it took members of Congress to travel to the capital. Franklin Roosevelt was the last president elected under the old system.

Roosevelt's first inaugural address was intended to boost the morale and

ROOSEVELT'S FIRST INAUGURAL ADDRESS: 1933

... So first of all, let me assert my firm belief that the only thing we have to fear is fear itself....

Our greatest primary task is to put people to work....

It can be accomplished in part by direct recruiting by the government itself ... [in order to accomplish] greatly needed projects to stimulate and reorganize the use of our natural resources....

We must act, and act quickly....

In our progress we require two safeguards against a return of the evils of the old order; there must be a strict supervision of all banking and credits and investments; there must be an end to speculation with other people's money; and there must be a provision for an adequate but sound currency....

I shall presently urge upon a new Congress in special session detailed measures for their fulfillment....

In the field of world policy, I would dedicate this nation to the policy of a good neighbor....

I shall ask the Congress for the one remaining instrument to meet the crisis —broad executive power to wage a war against the emergency as great as the power that would be given me if we were in fact invaded by a foreign foe....

We do not distrust the future of essential democracy. The people of the United States have not failed. In their need they have registered a mandate that they want direct, vigorous action.

They have asked for discipline and direction under leadership. They have made me the ... instrument of their wishes. In the spirit of the gift I take it....

hopes of a nation under the weight of a terrible economic depression. He assured the American people that the problems were solvable and that there was indeed much that the government could and would do to end the crisis. He spoke of banking reform and advocated a "good neighbor" policy in matters of world diplomacy.

During the period between March and June of his first term in office, President Roosevelt initiated his "New Deal." He began with a flurry of legislative activity, which he hoped would solve the immediate economic crisis and start the nation on its long road to full recovery.

BANKING REFORMS

On March 6, 1933, Roosevelt declared a four-day bank holiday, which would prevent the export and hoarding of gold or silver.

THE BANK HOLIDAY DECLARATION: 1933

... [I] do hereby proclaim ... that from Monday, the Sixth day of March, to Thursday, the Ninth day of March, Nineteen Hundred and Thirty-three, both dates inclusive, there shall be maintained and observed by all banking institutions and all branches thereof located in the United States of America, including the territories and insular possessions, a bank holiday, and that during said period all banking transactions shall be suspended....

During such holiday, [no bank] shall pay out, export, earmark, or permit the withdrawal or transfer [of any currency] whatsoever....

During a radio address, the president explained how the banking system worked, that money didn't stay where people deposited it, but that it was invested in many different forms. Under the Emergency Banking Relief Act, on March 9, only those banks that were fiscally sound were allowed to reopen. The Federal Deposit Insurance Corporation guaranteed bank deposits up to $5,000.

The president's quick action did much to restore faith in the banking system. It was not the end of the Great Depression, but it was the end of the downward spiral that had brought the economy to a standstill. Congress also passed legislation that would put people back to work. The Federal Emergency Relief Administration provided money to help those in need with food, clothing, and housing.

NEW DEAL ECONOMIC REFORMS

Soon after the First World War, Congress tried twice to pass legislation that would convert a hydroelectric plant and two munitions factories into facilities for peacetime use. But each time it was vetoed, first by President Calvin Coolidge and then by President Herbert Hoover. They both argued that because the plants would be government owned, it would be an example of socialism, something both men were against.

When Franklin D. Roosevelt became president, he believed the legislation would stimulate the

ROOSEVELT'S MESSAGE ON THE TENNESSEE VALLEY AUTHORITY: 1933

... I, therefore, suggest to the Congress legislation to create a Tennessee Valley Authority—a corporation clothed with the power of government but possessed of the flexibility and initiative of private enterprise. It should be charged with the broadest duty of planning for the proper use, conservation and development of the natural resources of the Tennessee River drainage basin and its adjoining territory for the general social and economic welfare of the nation....

▲ The Chickamauga Dam and powerhouse in Tennessee was one of the main Tennessee Valley Authority projects in 1933.

economy in one of the poorest regions of the United States, and he gave it his full support. As part of his New Deal, President Roosevelt asked Congress to set up the Tennessee Valley Authority (TVA) in May 1933. The munitions factory became a plant to manufacture fertilizers, and the hydroelectric plant generated power for parts of Virginia, North Carolina, Georgia, Tennessee, Kentucky, Alabama, and Mississippi.

But the development of the TVA upset many people. Representatives from private utility companies complained bitterly that a government agency shouldn't compete with their companies, especially when the cost of TVA power was lower than the rates they had been charging.

The thirty-four TVA dams on the Tennessee and Cumberland Rivers not only produced electric power but also aided in flood control and irrigation. The TVA also helped with reforestation and the preservation of wildlife.

The New Deal also enlarged the role the federal government played in agriculture. The Farm Credit Act of 1933 protected farmers against foreclosure on their property, while the Commodity Credit Corporation extended loans to farmers on their crops. The loans made to electrical cooperatives through the Rural Electrification Administration of 1935, doubled the number of farms receiving electricity by 1941.

The New Deal also expanded the government's role in industry. The National Industrial Recovery Act suspended antitrust laws and instituted codes of fair competition. It recognized the right of workers to form unions in order to engage in collective bargaining (negotiations between workers and employers). It established the 40-hour workweek, set a minimum weekly wage, and prohibited children under the age of sixteen from working.

However, some New Deal policies had to overcome a few challenges, including ones from the Supreme Court, which struck down the National Industrial Recovery Act and the Agricultural Adjustment Act, declaring some elements to be unconstitutional. Later laws were enacted to meet the court's objections.

Senator Huey Long of Louisiana, a potential rival of Roosevelt for the Democratic presidential nomination in 1940, developed his own "creative" economic recovery program, which he called "Share the Wealth."

SENATOR HUEY LONG'S "SHARE THE WEALTH" SPEECH: 1935

... 1. The fortunes of the multimillionaires and billionaires shall be reduced so that no one person shall own more than a few million dollars to the person....

3. ... We will throw into the government Treasury the money and property [from the rich] ... and with this money we will provide a home ... for every family in America, free of debt.

4. We guarantee ... employment for everyone ... by shortening the hours of labor to thirty hours per week ... and to eleven months per year....

5. We would provide education at the expense of the states and the United States for every child ... through ... college and vocational education....

6. We would give a pension to all person above sixty years of age....

7. Until we can straighten things out ... we would grant a moratorium on all debts which people owe that they cannot pay.

And now you have our program, none too big, none too little, but every man a king....

MORE FDR POLICIES

The Social Security Act of 1935 was a milestone that established old-age insurance under which workers who paid Social Security taxes on their wages would receive retirement benefits at age sixty-five.

The act also created several welfare programs, such as unemployment compensation and aid to needy children of single-parent families. Although it has proved to be the most enduring of the New Deal legislations, the act was very conservative. The government didn't pay for old-age benefits; workers and their employers did, but the tax was the same for everyone, which meant that the more workers earned, the less they were taxed proportionally. It also excluded a number of workers—most women, domestic servants, farm workers, and non-whites. Still, it was a highly significant development in social reform from Roosevelt's presidency.

During the Roosevelt years, there was also a change in the policy toward Indians. In 1933, the president appointed John Collier as head of the Bureau of Indian Affairs (BIA). After decades of corruption, land

fraud, and policies of assimilation, the BIA, under Collier's leadership, would finally see some reform. Collier's biggest contribution was

▲ One of President Roosevelt's most enduring policies was the Social Security Act, which he is shown signing in 1935.

pushing through the 1934 Indian Reorganization Act. Although Congress didn't approve all of Collier's suggestions, the act did contain three major changes.

The allotment program started under the Dawes Act came to an end, and all of the unsold Indian land was returned to the appropriate tribes. In addition, the federal government started a program that would repair and preserve Indian lands. Tribes were also allowed to set up political bodies to govern themselves, though they would still have to get the Secretary of the Interior's approval on most decisions. Indians would now receive special consideration for any open positions at the Bureau of Indians Affairs.

INDIAN REORGANIZATION ACT: 1934

... The Secretary of the Interior is hereby authorized ... to acquire ... land for Indians....

To proclaim ... [that] lands added to existing reservation[s] shall be designated for the exclusive use of Indians....

Any Indian tribe, or tribes, residing on the same reservation, shall have the right to organize for its common welfare, and may adopt an appropriate constitution and bylaws....

▲ Secretary of Interior Harold Ickes hands over the first constitution issued to delegates of the Flatland Indian Reservation.

REPEAL OF PROHIBITION

The Eighteenth Amendment, which banned the manufacture and sale of alcoholic beverages in the United States, was considered a failure from the moment it was ratified in January 1919, because of the opposition in large cities, the corruption of enforcement agents, and the lack of cooperation between state and federal officials.

In February 1933, Congress passed—and by December the required number of states had ratified —the Twenty-first Amendment, which repealed the Eighteenth. Control of liquor traffic reverted to the states. Almost immediately, local governments were inundated with requests for club liquor licenses, and law enforcement agencies had to work overtime to control a binge of public drinking.

ROOSEVELT IS REELECTED

In the presidential campaign of 1936, the Republican challenger, Governor Alf Landon of Kansas, denounced the Roosevelt administration for reckless experimentation and extravagant spending, but the president stood firm on his record. Roosevelt easily won the election, which he felt gave him a mandate to continue his sweeping social changes, but with war clouds gathering over Europe and the Japanese threat in the Pacific, President Roosevelt was forced to turn his attention to foreign policy.

ROOSEVELT'S SECOND INAUGURAL ADDRESS: 1937

… When four years ago we met to inaugurate a President, [we] pledged … to drive from the temple of our ancient faith those who had profaned it; to end by action, tireless and unafraid, the stagnation and despair of that day. We did those things first.…

But here is the challenge to our democracy: In this nation I see tens of millions of its

▲ President Roosevelt delivers his second inaugural address in 1937.

citizens—a substantial part of its whole population—who at this very moment are denied the greater part of what the lowest standards of today call the necessities of life.…

It is not in despair that I paint you that picture. I paint it in hope.…

Today we reconsecrate our country to long-cherished ideals in a suddenly changed civilization. In every land there are always at work forces that drive men apart and forces that drive men together. In our personal ambitions we are individualists. But in our seeking for economic and political progress as a nation, we all go up, or else we all go down, as one people.…

CHAPTER 3

Europe's War

1939–1941

During the 1920s, many nations around the world turned to Fascism. This political movement was characterized by ideas of national and racial superiority and dictatorial rule. In Germany, Adolf Hitler formed the Nazi party. Its members wanted Germany to be strong again after their defeat in World War I. By 1930, the Nazi party held the most seats in the Reichstag, the German parliament, and by 1933, Hitler was the undisputed leader of the country.

▲ Adolf Hitler and his Nazi aides view a parade in Nuremberg, Germany, in 1934.

In Italy, a politician named Benito Mussolini seized power and within a few years had created a Fascist dictatorship there. In Japan, another Fascist government was also coming to power. It promoted the belief that the Japanese people were superior to others and that strong nations had the right to conquer weaker ones.

All three Fascist powers—Germany, Italy, and Japan—wanted to expand their territory and were willing to fight wars to do so. Year by year, they became more aggressive. Japan had invaded China in 1931. In 1935, Italy invaded Ethiopia. In 1936, the German army moved into the Rhineland, an area of the country that was supposed to have no military forces, according to the Versailles Treaty. In 1938, Germany invaded Austria and the German-speaking area of Czechoslovakia.

In August 1939, Germany and the

… Tonight my single duty is to speak to the whole of America…. Until four-thirty this morning I had hoped against hope that some miracle would prevent a devastating war in Europe and bring to an end the invasion of Poland by Germany….

You must master at the outset a simple but unalterable fact in modern foreign relations between nations. When peace has been broken anywhere, the peace of all countries everywhere is in danger…. It is easy for you and for me to shrug our shoulders and to say that conflicts taking place thousands of miles from the continental United States … do not seriously affect … Americans … [but] every battle that is fought does affect the American future….

Let no man or woman thoughtlessly or falsely talk of America sending its armies to European fields. At this moment there is being prepared a proclamation of American neutrality…. I have said not once but many times that I have seen war and that I hate war. I say that again and again. I hope the United States will keep out of this war. I believe that it will. And I give you assurance and reassurance that every effort of your Government will be directed toward that end….

Soviet Union surprised the world by signing a nonaggression pact. In it, they agreed not to attack each other. With the Soviet Union no longer a threat, Germany invaded Poland on September 1. Great Britain and France could no longer sit by and watch as Hitler slowly took over Europe. They declared war on Germany. The Second World War had begun.

In a 1939 radio address, President Roosevelt quickly announced that the United States would remain neutral. He knew that most Americans wanted to stay out of the war, but he also knew that they had little sympathy for the Fascist regimes of Germany and Italy, so the Neutrality Act of 1939 permitted Great Britain and France to buy American arms and strategic materials, but they had to pay cash and to transport the goods in their own ships.

In the spring of 1940, after seven months in which no battles were fought, Germany invaded Denmark, Norway, the Netherlands, Belgium, Luxembourg, and France. Now Great Britain stood alone to face Hitler's military might. The United States knew it could no longer remain neutral. Fifty naval destroyers were sent to the British navy in exchange for leases to use British naval and air bases in Newfoundland, Bermuda, and British Guiana. With the Selective Service and Training Act, which instituted a draft, President Roosevelt hoped to have more than one million troops and eight hundred thousand reserves trained for military combat within a year. If war did come, and most people knew that it was only a matter of time, America would be ready to fight.

▲ A photograph, c.1942, shows a British destroyer patrolling the open seas.

FDR WINS A THIRD TERM IN OFFICE

No president had ever served more than two terms, but as the presidential election of 1940 approached, most Americans thought that Franklin D. Roosevelt was the only person who could lead the country in the perilous times to come. The Democratic Party convinced him to run for an unprecedented third term in office. Roosevelt easily won the election over the Republican candidate, Wendell Willkie, an Indiana lawyer and utilities executive. In his 1941 State of the Union address, the president gave one of his most enduring speeches. With war raging across Europe, he set forth his famous four freedoms.

ROOSEVELT'S STATE OF THE UNION ADDRESS: 1941

… Our national policy is this:

First, … we are committed to all-inclusive national defense.

Second, … we are committed to full support of all those resolute peoples, everywhere, who are resisting aggression and are thereby keeping war away from our hemisphere.…

Third, … we are committed to the proposition that principles of morality and considerations for our own security will never permit us to acquiesce in a peace dictated by aggressors and sponsored by appeasers.…

Therefore, the immediate need is a swift and driving increase in our armament production.… I … ask this Congress for authority and for funds sufficient to manufacture additional munitions and war supplies of many kind, to be turned over to those nations which are now in actual war with aggressor nations.…

In the future days, which we seek to make secure, we look forward to a world founded upon four essential human freedoms.

The first is freedom of speech and expression—everywhere in the world.

The second is freedom of every person to worship God in his own way—everywhere in the world.

The third is freedom from want … everywhere in the world.

The fourth is freedom from fear … everywhere in the world.…

This is no vision of a distant millennium. It is a definite basis for a kind of world attainable in our own time and generation.…

OURS... to fight for

Freedom of Speech

Freedom of Worship

Freedom from Want

Freedom from Fear

▲ A 1943 poster shows a series of paintings by Norman Rockwell that depict Roosevelt's four freedoms.

THE U.S. IS DRAWN INTO THE WAR

Although the U.S. would remain out of the war for a few months, it would still give Great Britain whatever it needed to defeat Nazi Germany.

Congress passed the Lend-Lease Act on March 11, 1941. This was the principal means of providing U.S. military aid to foreign nations. It authorized the president to transfer defense materials to the government of any country whose protection the president deemed vital to U.S. safety. After the unexpected German invasion of the Soviet Union in June, aid was also extended to that country in the form of military equipment.

In August 1941, President Roosevelt and Prime Minister Winston Churchill of Great Britain met for the first time in Argentia Bay off the coast of Newfoundland to issue a joint declaration on the purposes of the war against Fascism. Just as President Wilson's Fourteen Points had laid out America's post-war plans for World War I, the Atlantic Charter did the same for World War II.

Originally the Soviet Union, which had been attacked by Germany the month before, was to sign the charter as well, but the inclusion of the notion of "one world," in which nations abandoned their traditional beliefs in and reliance upon military alliances, did not appeal to Joseph Stalin. Churchill wasn't particularly interested, either, but Roosevelt, who had been a member of the Wilson administration, truly believed in the possibility of a world that would be governed by democratic processes, under the aegis of an international organization that would serve as an arbiter of disputes and protector of the peace—even though a similar organization, the League of Nations, had failed in the 1930s. In 1945, the Atlantic Charter would be the blueprint for the United Nations.

By the fall of 1941, the United States and Germany were fighting an undeclared naval war in the Atlantic, each country losing several ships.

On the other side of the world, in the Pacific, Japan saw American control of the Philippines as an obstacle to the expansion of its empire. For years, Japanese military leaders worked on different strategies to try to force the United States out of Asia. Finally, on November 3, 1941, the Japanese military approved Admiral Isoroku Yamamoto's plan to attack the United States Pacific Fleet, which was anchored at its Pearl Harbor naval base in Hawaii.

◀ President Roosevelt and British prime minister Winston Churchill meet in 1941.

THE ATLANTIC CHARTER: 1941

... First, [the United States and Great Britain] seek no aggrandizement, territorial or other....

Third, they respect the right of all peoples to choose the form of government under which they will live; and they wish to see sovereign rights and self government restored....

Fourth, they will endeavor ... to further the enjoyment by all States ... [of] the trade and [of] the raw materials of the world which are needed for their economic prosperity;

Fifth, they desire to bring about the fullest collaboration between all nations ... [to secure] economic advancement....

Sixth, after the final destruction of the Nazi tyranny, they hope to see ... a peace which will afford ... assurance that all men may live out their lives in freedom from fear and want....

Eighth, they believe that all of the nations of the world ... must come to the abandonment of the use of force ... [and] that the disarmament of such nations [which threaten aggression outside their borders] is essential....

"After the final destruction of the Nazi tyranny, they hope to see ... a peace."

CHAPTER 4

Roosevelt and World War II

1941–1945

On Sunday morning, December 7, 1941, the Japanese bombed the United States naval base at Pearl Harbor, Hawaii, in a surprise attack. It was the costliest naval defeat in American history. Nineteen ships—including three battleships—were either sunk or severely damaged. One hundred fifty planes were totally destroyed. More than twenty-three hundred soldiers and sailors were killed.

The next day, in a radio address heard around the world, President Roosevelt asked Congress for a formal declaration of war against the Empire of Japan. Three days later,

▲ The *U.S.S. West Virginia* burns after being hit by a bomb during the Japanese attack on Pearl Harbor.

FRANKLIN D. ROOSEVELT'S PEARL HARBOR ADDRESS: 1941

… Yesterday, December 7, 1941—a date which will live in infamy—the United States of America was suddenly and deliberately attacked by the naval and air forces of the Empire of Japan.…

It will be recorded that the distance of Hawaii from Japan makes it obvious that the attack was deliberately planned many days or even weeks ago.…

> The attack yesterday on the Hawaiian Island has caused severe damage to American naval and military forces. Very many American lives have been lost. In addition American ships have been reported torpedoed on the high seas between San Francisco and Honolulu....
>
> As commander in chief of the army and navy I have directed that all measures be taken for our defense....
>
> I ask that the Congress declare that since the unprovoked and dastardly attack by Japan on Sunday, December 7, a state of war has existed between the United States and the Japanese Empire....

on December 11, Germany and Italy declared war on the United States. The war in Europe and the war in Asia had become a global conflict.

THE WAR ON TWO FRONTS

Roosevelt knew that the United States could not fight an all-out war in two parts of the world at the same time, so the decision was made to concentrate first on defeating Germany.

In Europe, America's entry into the war boosted the morale of its Allies—Great Britain, France, and the Soviet Union. The Soviet Union kept asking the United States and Great Britain to open a second front as soon as possible with an Allied invasion of France. That way, the Russians hoped, the Germans would be forced to redistribute their forces, almost all of which were now fighting the Soviet Union. Remembering their heavy

casualties in France during the First World War, the British were reluctant to send their troops into Europe. In fact, an invasion across the English Channel was postponed several times.

In the interim, British and American troops forced the Germans out of North Africa and invaded Sicily and Italy. Soviet troops pushed westward into Eastern Europe. The military and diplomatic decisions made during this time would plant the seeds of the Cold War, with the Allies in control of Western Europe and the Russians in control of Eastern Europe.

The strategy against Japan, which evolved during 1942, was to use Australia as a base of operations to retake the Philippines and the southern coast of China, while at the same time destroying the Japanese navy and capturing the islands in the central Pacific.

WOMEN IN WORLD WAR II

Between 1941 and 1943, the number of women working outside the home grew by more than five million. Many of these women took nontraditional jobs in defense plants. "Rosie the Riveter," the symbol of all women factory workers, was one of the most enduring images of the American home front. Patriotism, a desire to get out of the house, and the chance to make extra money motivated the women, but even with the same level of experience at the same job, they received lower wages than men.

More than two hundred thousand women served in the military, primarily in the Women's Army Corps (WACs) or its navy counterpart, Women Accepted for Volunteer Emergency Service (WAVES). In 1942, Nancy Leftenant-Colon, a young black woman, had just begun her first year of nursing school when she saw a magazine photograph of an army nurse and decided to join up. In a 1998 interview, Leftenant-Colon talked about her struggles as the first black in the regular Army Nurse Corps.

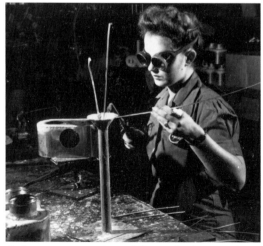
▲ A young woman welding a fuel pump in a U.S. aircraft plant during World War II.

LEFTENANT-COLON'S INTERVIEW: 1998

"Blacks just weren't Army nurses at the time."…

"It was like we were invisible to them."…

Although a racial divide separated the two camps of nurses, the black nurses began to develop a bond with their white patients.…

"It didn't seem to matter to the patients what color my skin was. Everybody bleeds red, after all.… The men always treated me with respect.… I guess it goes back to the way I was brought up. One of the things my father taught us was, 'Always treat a person the way you want to be treated.' I always tried to live by that rule."

JAPANESE-AMERICAN INTERNMENT CAMPS

After Pearl Harbor, Americans grew fearful that people within the country might help Japan. The long-held prejudices against Japanese living on the West Coast were only intensified by the attack, and President Roosevelt felt pressured by this anti-Japanese hysteria to take action. On February 19, 1942, he issued Executive Order 9066, which authorized the confinement of persons of Japanese ancestry from all areas of California, Oregon, and Washington that were considered possible targets of attack.

By September 1942, more than 110,000 Japanese men, women, and children—most of whom were American citizens—were uprooted from their homes, which they were forced to sell for a fraction of their value, and were placed in "relocation centers" in Arkansas, Arizona, California, Colorado, and Utah. These "centers" were merely rows of army-type barracks surrounded by barbed-wire fences. No comparable actions were taken against Americans of Italian or German descent.

In 1944, Fred Korematsu, a Japanese-American, challenged the constitutionality of the Japanese internment. Supreme Court Justice

EXECUTIVE ORDER 9066: 1942

... I hereby authorize and direct the Secretary of War ... to prescribe military areas in such places and of such extent as he or the appropriate Military Commanders may determine, from which any or all persons may be excluded ... for the ... control of alien enemies....

Hugo Black, writing the majority opinion of the court, said that military necessity justified the relocation. Although this opinion still stands today, the Civil Liberties Act of 1988 made some restitution to those individuals of Japanese ancestry who were interned during World War II.

▲ A Japanese-American family at the Manzanar Relocation Center in 1943.

JUSTICE HUGO BLACK'S OPINION IN *KOREMATSU* V. *UNITED STATES*: 1944

"The situation demanded that all citizens of Japanese ancestry be segregated from the West Coast temporarily."

The petitioner, an American citizen of Japanese descent, was convicted ... for remaining in ... a "Military Area," contrary to Civilian Exclusions Order No. 34....

To cast this case into outlines of racial prejudice, without reference to the real military dangers which were presented, merely confuses the issue. Korematsu was not excluded from the military area because of hostility to him or his race.... He was excluded because we are at war with the Japanese Empire, because the ... military authorities feared an invasion of our West Coast and felt constrained to take proper security measures, because they decided that ... the situation demanded that all citizens of Japanese ancestry be segregated from the West Coast temporarily, and finally, because Congress ... determined that they should have the power do just this.... We cannot—[in] ... the calm perspective of hindsight—now say that at the time these actions were unjustified....

THE D-DAY INVASION

On the eve of launching the greatest invasion in history, General Dwight D. Eisenhower, Supreme Commander of the Allied Forces in Europe, issued his "Orders of the Day," which was a rousing morale booster for the 175,000-member Allied expeditionary force. Shortly thereafter, in the early-morning hours of June 6, 1944—called D-Day—American, British, Canadian, and free-French forces stormed the beaches of Normandy in France, in what was known as "Operation Overlord."

This was the beginning of the end for the Axis powers—Germany, Italy, and Japan. Even though the Allies encountered stiff resistance at Normandy's Omaha Beach, the invasion surprised the German leaders, who had expected the attack to come at the narrower Channel crossing near the Pas de Calais. By July, Allied troops had secured the Normandy

GENERAL EISENHOWER'S D-DAY ORDERS: 1944

Soldier, Sailors and Airmen of the Allied Expeditionary Force!
You are about to embark upon the Great Crusade, toward which we have striven these many months. The eyes of the world are upon you. The hopes and prayers of liberty-loving people everywhere march with you. In company with our brave Allies and brothers-in-arms on other Fronts, you will bring about the destruction of the German war machine, the elimination of Nazi tyranny over the oppressed peoples of Europe, and security for ourselves in a free world. Your task will not be an easy one. Your enemy is well trained, well equipped and battle-hardened.... Our Home Fronts have given us an overwhelming superiority in weapons and munitions of war, and placed at our disposal great reserves of trained fighting men. The tides has turned! The free men of the world are marching together to Victory! I have full confidence in your courage, devotion to duty and skill in battle. We will accept nothing less than full Victory! Good luck!...

beaches and were headed for Paris, which they liberated in August.

By September, the Allies had pushed the German forces out of both France and Belgium, but in December, the Germans counter-attacked through Belgium. The resulting battle was called the "Battle of the Bulge," because the German army pushed a "bulge" through the American and British lines.

Hitler hoped the battle would give his scientists time to finish their atomic weapons, which he planned to use on Great Britain, but the Allies

▲ American troops about to hit the beach in the D-Day invasion on June 6, 1944.

counterattacked and, after ten days of the heaviest fighting of the war, the German troops retreated into Germany. During the battle, Eduardo A. Peniche, an American soldier in the 502nd Infantry, wrote some notes in a journal, so he would always remember what happened during that time.

EDUARDO A. PENICHE'S JOURNAL: 1944

Thursday, December 21st: … We woke up with a heavy blanket of snow [that] was making us feel miserably uncomfortable…. O'Toole told us that the word from [headquarters] was to conserve our ammunition and our rations….

Friday, December 22nd: … The heavy blanket of snow covered our entire sector and we were surrounded by the enemy…. It was incredibly cold; the water in our canteens was freezing. We also have to rub each other's feet to prevent frostbite…. I was terrified by the thought of freezing to death….

Sunday, December 24th: … We were told that the enemy had given [General McCauliffe] an ultimatum to surrender but [he had refused]. We all got a big kick when we heard that [he] had said "NUTS" to the enemy….

❝I was terrified by the thought of freezing to death.❞

THE WAR IN EUROPE ENDS

By the end of January 1945, British and American forces had crossed the Rhine River, invading Germany from the west. At the same time, Russian troops had crossed Poland and were invading Germany from the east.

Three times during the war, the leaders of the United States, Great Britain, and the Soviet Union met to discuss global issues. The most important conference was the second one, which took place at the Soviet Crimea resort of Yalta in February 1945. At the time, Germany was already on the edge of defeat, and the three Allied powers wanted to make plans for the post-war world. A set of agreements was worked out. The most important ones concerned the founding of the United Nations, what the Soviet Union's role would be in the war against Japan, and how Germany would be divided.

On April 12, President Roosevelt, whose health had been failing, died, and it was left to his vice president, Harry S. Truman, to bring the nation to victory in Europe and the Pacific. On April 30, Adolf Hitler killed himself in his underground bunker. Admiral Karl Dönitz, whom Hitler had named as his successor, surrendered to General Eisenhower at Reims, France, on May 7.

THE YALTA CONFERENCE: 1945

… A United Nations conference on the proposed world organization should be summoned for Wednesday, 25 April, 1945, and should be held in the United States of America.…

The United Kingdom, the United States of America, and the Union of Soviet Socialist Republics shall possess supreme authority with respect to Germany.…

It was agreed that a zone in Germany, to be occupied by the French forces, should be allocated France. This zone would be formed out of the British and American zones.…

The conference agreed that the question of the major war criminals should be the subject of inquiry by the three Foreign Secretaries for report in due course after the close of the conference.…

◀ Prime Minister Churchill *(left)*, President Roosevelt *(center)*, and the Soviet marshal Joseph Stalin *(right)* meet in Yalta.

THE HOLOCAUST

As Allied troops marched into Germany and Poland, they made a horrifying discovery. The Nazis had murdered millions of Jews in concentration camps at Dachau, Auschwitz, Buchenwald, and many other places, and their remains were burned in huge ovens.

The Nazis called this program of extermination the "final solution" to their "Jewish problem." The world remembers it as the "Holocaust." Dorothy Wahlstrom was a captain with a hospital unit that entered the Dachau concentration camp, outside Munich, Germany. In 1990, she wrote a chapter in the book *Witnesses to the Holocaust*, describing the grizzly sights they saw upon entering the camp.

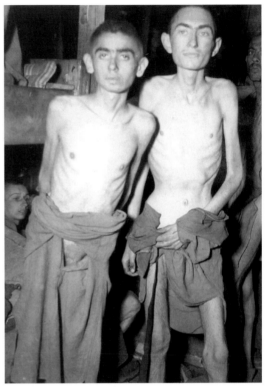

▲ In May 1945, prisoners in the Amphing concentration camp in Germany were liberated by U.S. troops.

WITNESSES TO THE HOLOCAUST: 1990

...The dead and dying were all around us. Piles of naked dead were stacked beside the crematorium and inside. Dachau was certainly a calculated attempt by the Nazis to desecrate not only the body, but also the mind and spirit.

We set up ward units in the S.S. barracks. Dead dogs lay in the kennels nearby, killed by our military after survivors told us they were used to tear away parts of prisoners' bodies on command.... They told us that prisoners who could no longer work were used as live targets for machine gun practice. They mentioned other unspeakable atrocities—medical experiments, torture chambers—horrors too terrible to think up without having experienced them....

THE ATOMIC AGE BEGINS

In 1939, physicist Albert Einstein wrote a letter to President Roosevelt, telling him that Germany was developing a single bomb that could easily destroy an entire city. When the president was informed that an atomic bomb was now a very real possibility, he created the Manhattan Project for the purpose of making such a bomb for the United States' military arsenal. It would be the nation's most expensive and top-secret military program ever, and by 1945, it would also produce the world's first atomic bomb.

ALBERT EINSTEIN'S LETTER TO PRESIDENT ROOSEVELT: 1939

... Some recent work by E. Fermi and L. Szilard ... leads me to expect that the element uranium may be turned into a new and important source of energy....

This new phenomenon would also lead to the construction of ... extremely powerful bombs of a new type.... A single bomb of this type, carried by boat and exploded in a port, might very well destroy the whole port together with some of the surrounding territory....

The United States has only very poor ores of uranium in moderate quantities. There is some good ore in Canada and the former Czechoslovakia, while the most important source of uranium is [in the] Belgian Congo.

In view of this situation you may think it desirable to have some permanent contact maintained between the Administration and the group of physicists working on chain reactions in America....

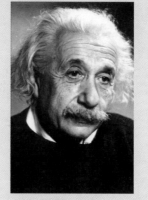

▲ A 1946 photograph of physicist Albert Einstein.

"This new phenomenon would also lead to the construction of ... extremely powerful bombs of a new type."

THE WAR IN THE PACIFIC ENDS

In May 1942, the tide of war in the Pacific turned in favor of the Allies, as they halted the Japanese advance at the Battle of the Coral Sea, which prevented an invasion of Australia.

In June, the American and Japanese navies fought one of the greatest naval battles in history off the island of Midway, which ended Japan's threat to Hawaii. Following that, U.S. Marines won the Japanese occupied Pacific islands of Guadalcanal and Tarawa. In October 1944, General Douglas MacArthur defeated almost the entire Japanese navy at the Battle of Leyte Gulf, leading to the recapture of the Philippines, which had been lost in 1942. In early 1945, Americans successfully invaded Iwo Jima and Okinawa, Japanese islands on which there were military bases. As the Allied forces moved closer to Japan, the Japanese military launched *kamikaze* attacks (suicide attacks), in which pilots in airplanes loaded with explosives crashed into American warships.

To hasten the end of the war in the Pacific, President Truman authorized the dropping of an atomic bomb on the Japanese city of Hiroshima, which was chosen for several reasons.

TRUMAN'S RADIO ADDRESS: 1945

... Sixteen hours ago an American airplane dropped one bomb on Hiroshima, an important Japanese army base. That bomb had more power than twenty thousand tons of TNT....

We are now prepared to obliterate more rapidly and completely every productive enterprise the Japanese have above ground in any city. We shall destroy their docks, their factories, and their communications. Let there be no mistake; we shall completely destroy Japan's power to make war....

It was an important commercial and manufacturing center with a large army base. It had also never been bombed before, which would not only allow scientists to study the power of the explosion but demonstrate the resolve of the United States to use nuclear weapons against the Japanese in order to save the lives of thousands of American soldiers. In a radio address, Truman announced his decision to use the bomb.

The bomb destroyed more than

▲ A 1945 photograph of the mushroom-cloud atomic bomb dropped on Nagasaki, Japan.

four square miles of the city, killing more than seventy thousand people. Three days later, a second bomb was dropped on Nagasaki, causing about forty thousand deaths. The Japanese government surrendered on August 15.

Isao Kita, a weatherman for the Hiroshima Weather Bureau, was thirty-three years old when the atomic bomb was dropped on Hiroshima. In 1986, he gave an account of what happened when the bomb exploded.

TESTIMONY OF ISAO KITA: 1986

… I was in the receiving room, and I was facing northward. I noticed the flashing light…. In a few seconds, the heat wave arrived…. By that time, I realized that the bomb had been dropped…. There is a path … by [the weather bureau]. [I saw] a large number of injured persons walk[ing] toward the Omi Hospital. The were bleeding all over and some of them had no clothes…. When I looked down on the town … I could see that the city was completely lost. The city [had] turned into a yellow sand. It turned yellow, the color of the yellow desert….

CHAPTER 5

Truman's Post-War America

1945–1949

With the atomic bomb in its possession and an economy made strong by World War II, the United States was now the most powerful nation in the world, but tensions with the Soviet Union turned into the conflict known as the "Cold War." Americans were now worried about Communism (a system of government under which all property is owned by the state) instead of Fascism. During the Cold War, the United States and the Soviet Union each worked to influence smaller countries against the other, while each also built up its own military to intimidate the other. Americans were now worried about Communists instead of Fascists. Underlying the struggle for world leadership between the Western Allies led by the United States and the Communist bloc nations led by the Soviet Union was the knowledge that if the Cold War ever erupted, it would be an atomic war that could destroy the world.

In February 1946, after Stalin gave a speech in which he said that the main threat to the world was capitalism (a system of government that promotes private ownership of production and distribution of goods and services), George F. Kennan, the chargé d'affaires at the American

GEORGE KENNAN'S TELEGRAM TO WASHINGTON: 1946

… We have here a political force committed fanatically to the belief that with US there can be no permanent modus vivendi, that it is desirable and necessary that the internal harmony of our society be disrupted, our traditional way of life be destroyed, the international authority of our state be broken, if Soviet power to be to secure. The political force has complete power of disposition over energies of one of the world's greatest peoples and resources of the world's richest national territory, and is borne along by a deep and powerful current of Russian nationalism. In addition, it has an elaborate and far-flung apparatus for exertion of its influence in other countries, an apparatus of amazing flexibility and versatility, managed by people whose experience and skill in underground methods are presumably without parallel in history. Finally it is seemingly inaccessible to considerations of reality in its basic reactions....

The problem of how to cope with this force is [the] greatest task our diplomacy has ever faced and probably the greatest it will ever have to face....

But I would like to record my conviction that the problem is within our power to solve—and that without recourse to any general military conflict....

[The Soviet Union], unlike ... [Hitler's] Germany, is neither schematic nor adventuristic.... It does not take unnecessary risks....

Embassy in Moscow, sent a telegram to the State Department in Washington, D.C. He said that while Stalin's beliefs made normal relations with the Soviet Union almost impossible, he believed that firmness on the part of the United States and its Allies could contain Soviet ambitions in other parts of the world.

CHURCHILL WARNS AGAINST SOVIET POWER

In 1945, the war-weary people of Great Britain voted Winston Churchill out of office. Because some American politicians had begun advocating closer ties to the Soviet Union (against Kennan's advice), the British government now felt isolated and under pressure from the Soviets in many places, such as Iran, the Balkans, and the Mediterranean. No one felt this more than Churchill. The two central themes of his career were opposition to Communism and gaining U.S. support for the goals of British foreign policy. To see the United States drifting toward a friendlier relationship with the Soviet Union was distressing.

On March 5, 1946, at the encouragement of President Truman, Churchill delivered a speech—"Sinews of Peace"—in Fulton, Missouri, in which he talked about forming an Anglo-American partnership to block Soviet expansion. This speech became one of the landmark statements of the Cold War.

Former prime minister Winston Churchill and President Truman arrive in Fulton, Missouri in 1946, where Churchill delivered his "Sinews of Peace" speech. ▶

WINSTON CHURCHILL'S "SINEWS OF PEACE" ADDRESS IN FULTON, MISSOURI: 1946

… Neither the sure prevention of war, nor the continued rise of world organization will be gained without what I have called the fraternal association of the English-speaking peoples. This means a special relationship between the British Commonwealth and Empire and the United States.…

A shadow has fallen upon the scenes so lately lighted by the Allied victory.…

From Stettin in the Baltic to Trieste in the Adriatic, an iron curtain has descended across the Continent … and the populations … lie in what I must call the Soviet sphere, and all are subject in one form or another, not only to Soviet influence but to a very high and, in many cases, increasing measure of control from Moscow.…

From what I have seen of our Russian friends and Allies during the war, I am convinced that there is nothing they admire so much as strength, and there is nothing for which they have less respect than for weakness, especially military weakness.…

In September 1946, Nikolai Novikov, the Soviet ambassador in Washington, D.C., drafted a telegram to his superiors in Moscow—in much the same way that George F. Kennan had done in his long telegram to the Department of State earlier that year—to try to explain the foreign policy of the United States.

Kennan believed that in order for the Soviet Union to maintain its authoritarian power, the Soviets would wage a patient but deadly struggle to extend their Communist reach to other countries. Therefore, he felt the best way to deal with the Soviet Union was to develop a diplomatic strategy that would keep the Soviets from bringing other countries into the Communist bloc.

In contrast to Kennan's beliefs, Novikov stressed that the United States was striving for world supremacy through its imperialist tendencies of capitalism. He claimed that capitalism was "infiltrating" the economies of other nations. He also cited evidence that the United States was building up its military presence all around the world—with some bases very close to the borders of the Soviet Union.

The intense distrust between the United States and the Soviet Union

THE NOVIKOV TELEGRAM: 1946

... The foreign policy of the United States, which reflects the imperialist tendencies of American monopolistic capital, is characterized in the postwar period by a striving for world supremacy. This is the real meaning of the many statements by President Truman and other representatives of American ruling circles; that the United States has the right to lead the world. All the forces of American diplomacy—the army, the air force, the navy, industry, and science—are enlisted in the service of this foreign policy. For this purpose broad plans for expansion have been developed and are being implemented through diplomacy and the establishment of a system of naval and air bases stretching far beyond the boundaries of the United States, through the arms race, and through the creation of even newer types of weapons....

eventually led to a massive buildup of nuclear arms over a period of several decades in both countries.

THE TRUMAN DOCTRINE

In 1946, a civil war broke out in Greece between Communist factions and the British-supported government. At the same time, the Soviet Union began pressuring Turkey to let it build naval bases on that country's northwestern coast.

When Great Britain no longer had the resources to help these two countries meet the growing Soviet threats, President Truman told Congress that if the United States didn't do something to help Greece and Turkey, disorder could spread throughout the entire region and even spill over into the Middle East. At issue, Truman insisted, was the very security of the United States. In a speech later known as the Truman Doctrine, the president stated that the United States would support free peoples who were resisting attempted subjugation by armed minorities or by outside pressures.

THE TRUMAN DOCTRINE: 1947

... The United States has received from the Greek Government an urgent appeal for financial and economic assistance....

The very existence of the Greek state is today threatened by the terrorist activities of several thousand armed men, led by the Communists....

Greece's neighbor, Turkey, also deserves our attention....

I therefore ask the Congress to provide authority for assistance to Greece and Turkey in the amount of $400,000,000 for the period ending June 30, 1948....

In addition to funds, I ask the Congress to authorize the detail of American civilian and military personnel to Greece and Turkey, at the request of those countries, to assist in the tasks of reconstruction, and for the purpose of supervising the use of such financial and material assistance as may be furnished....

The free peoples of the world look to us for support in maintaining their freedoms. If we falter in our leadership, we may endanger the peace of the world—and we shall surely endanger the welfare of our own nation....

THE MARSHALL PLAN

Two years after the end of the Second World War, most of Europe still lay in ruins. All the countries were struggling to rebuild, but France and Italy also faced the growing strength of their local Communist parties. On June 5, 1947, Secretary of State George Marshall outlined his extensive plan for recovery. It would begin by pumping $13 billion into the countries of Western Europe to help them rebuild. The Marshall Plan was later extended to Japan, South Korea, and Taiwan.

By rebuilding these countries quickly, the United States could end the long-term dependence on aid that these countries relied on, and they could be restored as trading partners. Germany, Europe's most industrialized and resource-rich country, was

▲ A poster promoting the European Recovery Program (the Marshall Plan) in Europe.

THE MARSHALL PLAN: 1947

... The truth of the matter is that Europe's requirements for the next three or four years for foreign food and other essential products ... are so much greater than her present ability to pay that she must have substantial additional help, or face economic, social, and political deterioration....

It is logical that the United States should do whatever it is able to do to assist in the return of normal economic health to the world, without which there can be no political stability and no assured peace. Our policy is directed not against any country or doctrine but against hunger, poverty, desperation, and chaos. Its purpose should be the revival of working economy in the world so as to permit the emergence of political and social conditions in which free institutions can exist....

particularly important in this effort. The Marshall Plan also fostered a willingness on the part of these nations to help the United States fight Communism.

NATO Is Established

In 1948, when Britain, France, and the United States started to merge their occupation zones to form the country of West Germany, the Soviet Union blocked all access to Berlin and what would soon be known as East Germany. Truman saw that the United States needed a Western security pact.

In April1 1949, the United States and Canada, along with several European nations, founded the North Atlantic Treaty Organization (NATO). Not since 1778 had the United States entered into a formal European military alliance. Some critics argued that it would provoke war rather than deter it. Truman countered that NATO would function as a "trip wire," bringing the full force of the United States to bear on the Soviet Union if it ever attacked Western Europe. Truman also hoped that NATO would keep Western Europeans from embracing Communism or even neutralism in the Cold War. The United States Senate ratified the treaty by eighty-two votes to thirteen.

In 1952, NATO expanded to include the countries of Greece and Turkey. When West Germany was admitted in 1955, the Soviet Union countered by establishing the Warsaw Pact, a military alliance of Eastern European Communist countries, including East Germany, that would be prepared to fight any perceived NATO aggression.

THE NORTH ATLANTIC TREATY: 1949

... The Parties [the United States, Canada, Great Britain, France, Italy, Belgium, the Netherlands, Luxembourg, Portugal, Denmark, Norway, and Iceland] agree that an armed attack against one or more of them in Europe or North America shall be considered an attack against them all, and consequently they agree that, if such an armed attack occurs, each of them, in exercise of the right of individual or collective self defense recognized by Article 51 of the Charter of the United Nations, will assist the Party or Parties so attacked by taking forthwith, individually, and in concert with the other Parties, such action as it deems necessary, including the use of armed force, to restore and maintain the security of the North Atlantic area....

LABOR UNREST

When wartime price controls ended in mid-1946, there was a nearly twenty-five percent increase in the cost of certain things—especially food. In response, almost five million workers across the country went on strike for higher wages, a move that President Truman thought would bring the country to a standstill.

He ordered the federal government to seize the coal mines and even threatened to draft striking railroad workers into the army (which he never did), but his actions cost the Democrats their labor support, and in the mid-term elections, the Republicans won control of Congress.

Unlike Truman, who was pro-labor but opposed to union decisions that he thought would harm the nation's economy, the Republicans were anti-labor. They immediately passed the Taft-Hartley Act—over Truman's veto—which restricted what labor unions could do. This act was a major setback for the labor movement. In effect, labor union anger at Truman and the Democratic party backfired.

TRUMAN IS REELECTED

In the 1948 presidential campaign, the Democratic party was up against more than the Republicans, who had nominated Thomas E. Dewey, the governor of New York, as their candidate. Henry A. Wallace became the Progressive party's candidate, advocating friendly relations with the Soviet Union, racial desegregation, and nationalization of basic industries. A fourth party, known as the Dixiecrats, was organized by Southerners who walked out of the Democratic convention when the party adopted a pro–civil rights plank. Truman's chances looked bleak.

Truman embarked on an exhausting campaign across the country, and in what some people considered an upset, he won the election. But within a few months, America was once again embroiled in another war.

▲ A victorious Truman holds up the *Chicago Daily Tribune* with the incorrect headline "Dewey Defeats Truman."

TIME LINE

1929	■ The stock market crashes, beginning the Great Depression.
1932	■ Franklin Roosevelt is elected the thirty-second U.S. president.
1933	■ New Deal recovery measures are enacted by Congress.
1933	■ The Twenty-first Amendment to the Constitution repeals Prohibition.
1935	■ The Works Progress Administration (WPA) is established with the goal of putting Americans back to work.
1935	■ The Social Security Act is passed.
1939	■ World War II begins in Europe.
1941	■ Japan bombs Pearl Harbor; the U.S. declares war on Japan;
1941	■ Germany and Italy declare war on the United States.
1942	■ Executive Order 9066 authorizes internment of Japanese-American citizens.
1942–1943	■ The Allies invade North Africa and Italy.
1944	■ The Allies conduct the D-Day invasion of France.
1945	■ Roosevelt, Churchill, and Stalin meet at Yalta to discuss the post-war occupation of Germany.
1945	■ President Roosevelt dies of a stroke and is succeeded by Vice President Harry. S. Truman, the thirty-third U.S. president.
1945	■ Germany surrenders to the Allies.
1945	■ Allied troops discover the death camps where millions of Jews were exterminated.
1945	■ The United States drops an atomic bomb on Hiroshima, Japan, and a few days later drops another bomb on Nagasaki.
1945	■ Japan agrees to unconditional surrender.
1947	■ The Marshall Plan for European post-war recovery is outlined.
1948	■ Truman is elected for a second term as president.
1949	■ The North Atlantic Treaty Organization (NATO) is established.

GLOSSARY

Allied powers: in World War II, primarily Great Britain, Russia, and the United States.

Axis powers: in World War II, Germany, Italy, and Japan

Bonus Army: World War I veterans who marched on Washington, D.C., in 1932 demanding their pensions.

capitalism: economic system characterized by open competition.

civil liberties: rights and privileges of ordinary citizens.

Cold War: non-military struggle mostly between the United States and the Soviet Union for world domination between 1945 and 1991.

Communism: social system in which everything is owned by the state.

D-Day: in World War II, the day when Allied forces invaded France.

draft: compulsory enlistment into military service.

Executive order: command given by the president.

extermination: the act of destroying something or someone completely.

Fascism: a type of government that is characterized by dictatorial rule.

gross national product: total value of all goods produced by a nation.

Holocaust: slaughter of European Jews by Nazi Germany during World War II.

Hooverville: name given to the poor parts of towns when Herbert Hoover was president.

hydroelectric plant: place where electricity is generated by running water.

internment camp: place where people are confined, especially during wartime.

kamikaze: a Japanese attack by a "suicide pilot" during World War II.

munitions: war weapons.

Nazi: member of political party that ruled Germany from 1933 to 1945.

New Deal: the group of social programs started by President Franklin Roosevelt to help Americans recover from the Great Depression.

Rosie the Riveter: fictional name for all American women working in factories during World War II.

sinews: sources of strength of a person or a nation.

Social Security: U.S. government program that provides financial help to people.

union: a group of workers united for their common good.

veterans: men or women who have served in the U.S. military.

WAC: in World War II, the Women's Army Corp.

WAVES: in World War II, Women Accepted for Volunteer Emergency Service, the women's reserve of the U.S. Navy.

FURTHER INFORMATION

BOOKS

Opdyke, Irene Gut. *In My Hands: Memories of a Holocaust Rescuer.* Alfred A. Knopf, Inc., 1999.

Uys, Errol Lincoln. *Riding the Rails: Teenagers on the Move During the Great Depression.* Routledge, 1999.

Werner, Emmy E. *Through the Eyes of Innocents: Children Witness World War II.* Westview Press, 2001.

WEB SITES

www.historyplace.com/unitedstates/pacificwar/index.html An award-winning Web site that presents a detailed time line of World War II in the Pacific. There are also selected photos of many of the battles fought there.

www.pbs.org/wgbh/amex/rails/timeline/ This Web site by PBS (Public Broadcasting Service) presents a detailed time line on the Great Depression and covers the years from 1929 to 1940.

USEFUL ADDRESSES

United States Holocaust Memorial Museum
100 Raoul Wallenberg Place, SW
Washington, DC 20024
Telephone: (202) 488–0400

National World War II Memorial
900 Ohio Drive SW
Washington, DC 20024
Telephone (202) 426-6841

★ ★ ★ INDEX ★ ★ ★